CONTEMPORARY'S ACTIVITY-BASED EMPLOYMENT PROGRAM

You're Hired!

Book One: Charting Your Career Path

Marilyn Clark
John Mahaffy
Michael St. John
Jan Hart Weihmann

Project Editor
Sarah Conroy

Consultant
**Maryann D. Sakamoto
Assistant Principal/Adult Education
Atlantic County Vocational School
Mays Landing, New Jersey**

CB
CONTEMPORARY
BOOKS
CHICAGO

Library of Congress Cataloging-in-Publication Data

You're hired! / Marilyn Clark . . . [et al.].
      p.   cm.
     Contents: Bk. 1. Charting your career path.
     ISBN 0-8092-4031-9
      1. Vocational guidance.   I. Clark, Marilyn.
HF5381.Y69   1991
650.14—dc20   91-23647
                                CIP

Photo Credits: p. 1—© Comstock Inc., Peter D'Angelo; p. 4—© Larry Lefever/Grant Heilman Photography; p. 11—© Dwight Cendrowski/Telephoto; pp. 14, 35, 53—© C. C. Cain Photography; p. 36—Chicago Citywide Colleges/Office of Public Information; p. 61—City Colleges of Chicago

Published by Contemporary Books, Inc.
Two Prudential Plaza, Chicago, Illinois 60601-6790
Manufactured in the United States of America
International Standard Book Number: 0-8092-4031-9

Published simultaneously in Canada by
Fitzhenry & Whiteside
195 Allstate Parkway
Markham, Ontario L3R 4T8
Canada

Editorial Director Caren Van Slyke	*Cover Design* Georgene Sainati
Editorial Mark Boone Betsy Rubin Jane Samuelson Lisa Black Eunice Hoshizaki Laura E. Larson Lynn McEwan	*Cover Illustrator* Linda Kelen *Illustrator* Graziano, Krafft & Zale, Inc. *Art & Production* Carolyn Hopp
Editorial Assistant Erica Pochis	*Typography* Ellen Yukel
Editorial Production Manager Norma Fioretti	*Photo Research* Sheryl Mersfelder
Production Editor Jean Farley Brown	*Photography* C. C. Cain
Production Assistant Marina Micari	

Contents

To the Student

This is the first of two books in the series *You're Hired!*
This book, *Charting Your Career Path*, will help you learn
more about yourself and the jobs that may be best for you.
Book Two, *Getting the Right Job*, will help you learn how
to find and keep the job that's right for you.

 ## Charting Your Career Path

Many people think a job is just about making money. If it
pays well, it must be good. But this may not be true for
you. To have a successful career, you must have a job that
matches most of your own values, skills, and interests.

If you know about yourself and what you need from a job,
you can make better choices. The better a job fits you, the
more successful you will be. This book focuses on you and
on the kind of work that is right for you.

What you will learn:

- what is important to you

- how to solve problems

- how to find information about jobs

- new words

- how to make good decisions about jobs

How you will learn:

- by reading stories and answering questions

- by using your community as a resource

- by doing activities about your values, skills, and
  interests

As you work through this book, remember that there are
few right or wrong answers. The **best** answer is the one
that is right for you. You should check with your teacher
often to be sure you are on the right track.

VALUES
UNIT ONE

What's Important to You?

Work is an important part of your **career** and your life. A career is more than a job, or the work you do for pay. A career includes your **values**. It includes the time you spend doing things that are important to you. Since you want to make choices about your future career, now is a good time to think about your values—the things you care about.

How This Unit Will Help You

You have values you want to live by. Knowing more about your values will help you make good choices about your life and career.

In this unit you will

■ learn what you **value** most

■ decide which of your **values** comes first

■ discover what your **values** say about the kinds of jobs you may like

■ write a **summary** of your values

What Do You Value?

To choose a career you will be happy with, you need to understand your own values. You can discover some of your values by thinking about how you like to spend your time. What kinds of people, places, and activities do you like the best?

There are three different types of values.

1. Personal Values

Some things are important for you to have in your life, just because of who you are. Each person has a different set of values. If it is important to you to *be in good shape*, you may not be happy in a job where you have to sit at a desk all day. You need to consider your **personal values** before you make career decisions.

2. Work Values

Some jobs may seem interesting to you, and other jobs may not sound good at all. Your **work values** have to do with the things that are most important to you in a job. For instance, it may be important to you to *work with other people*, or *work close to home*.

3. People Values

Your **people values** have to do with how you deal with other people. It may be important to you to *meet new people* or to *help others*. Understanding your people values will help you choose a job you will enjoy.

To see more examples, look at the three values lists on the following page.

■ Values

Look at the three values lists below. If you would like, add other values to these lists.

PERSONAL VALUES
Be free to do what I
  enjoy
Be happy
Sense of inner peace
Feel good about myself
Have good health
Be liked by others
Have fun in my life
Have no worries about
  money
Know I did well
Have lots of free time
Be in good shape
Be loving
Be kind to others
Be in charge of my
  own life
Be honest
Do what I know I
  should
Have others respect me
Live in a certain part
  of the country
Have an open mind
Be neat
Take risks
Have time to think
Be artistic

WORK VALUES
Have steady work
Earn good money
Work indoors
Work outdoors
Travel for my work
Work the same hours
  every day
Have friends on the job
Have a good boss
Help others
Be part of a team
Learn new things
Know what I am
  supposed to do
Work flexible hours
Be in charge
Do or make something
  important
Work with people
Feel good about my
  work
Work close to home
Do one thing at a time
Work in my own way
Stay busy
Work by myself
Do clean work
Get ahead in my job
Have health insurance
Have vacation and sick
  days
Do many different
  things
Use what I already
  know

PEOPLE VALUES
Have lots of friends
Have close family ties
Know lots of people
Have a good, solid
  marriage
Have someone to turn
  to or talk to
Make friends
Be needed
Have a few close
  friends
Have family nearby
Have time to be alone
Know people I can
  trust
Have a great social life
Spend money on my
  friends
Have someone to do
  things with
Be a good friend
Be a good parent
Be a good son or
  daughter
Help others
Meet new people
Be independent

Tom's Story

Tom worked at Sam's Meat Market. Sam was a good boss, but he could not pay very high wages because business was slow. The men worked hard. Sam was the meat cutter. Tom kept the cases stocked and cleaned. He also cleaned the store and the back room. Both men sold the meat. They weighed and packed the meat for customers. Tom liked the work.

This job was important to Tom for two reasons. First, his wife was going to have a baby. Second, even if he did not make much money now, Tom felt that someday he could buy the business from Sam.

But Tom needed more money, so he got a second job. He worked four hours pumping gas after he left the meat market. The money from the job at the gas station meant that they could pay all their bills.

Tom's wife wanted him to spend a lot of time at home after the baby was born. Tom knew that they would need a larger apartment very soon.

Just after the baby was born, Sam got sick. He needed Tom to work two or three more hours every day, but he could pay him for only one more hour. He also said that he liked Tom's work, and that this was a good chance for Tom to learn more about the meat market business.

When Tom told his wife, she said that they needed the bigger apartment soon. She also said that he must spend more time with the baby. Tom felt the same way. He began to worry.

Questions About the Story

Use the list of values on page 3 to help you answer the questions below.

1. What **personal** values do you think Tom has?

_____

_____

_____

2. What **work** values do you think Tom has?

_____

_____

_____

3. What **people** values do you think Tom has?

_____

_____

_____

How do you think Tom will work things out? You may want to talk with someone in your class about Tom's choices.

Answers

1., 2., and 3., answers will vary

Sorting Out Your Own Values

Now that you have looked at someone else's values, it is time to look at your own. Because these are *your* values, there are no right or wrong answers. You will sort three decks of cards. Be sure to finish sorting one deck before going on to the next.

You may need more than one class period to do this.

Card Sort Directions

Step 1. Look at page 77 in this book. Pages 77–92 can be torn out and cut to make cards. Most cards will look something like this:

■ PERSONAL VALUES ■

Be happy

       a. Find a large flat surface, like a table or the floor.

       b. Find the three cards that say YES, MAYBE, and NO. Cut these cards out, and set them aside.

       c. Find the three cards that say **Must have it**, **Nice to have it**, and **Can get along without it**. Set these cards aside also.

       d. Tear out the rest of the cards and make three decks—one for each type of value.

Note: If you would like to add new values to the card decks, write the new values on the blank cards provided on pages 81, 87, and 91.

Step 2. Put the YES, MAYBE, and NO cards across the top of the space in front of you— like this:

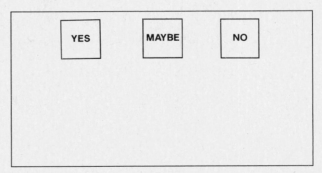

YES   MAYBE   NO

Step 3. Pick up the **Personal Values** deck of cards.

   a. Read the value on the first card. Think about how important that value is to you. Go with your first thought about each value.

     ■ If it is **very important**, place the card below the YES card.

     ■ If it is **somewhat important** to you, place the card below the MAYBE card.

     ■ If it is **not important** to you, place the card below the NO card.

   b. Now sort the rest of the deck. After you have sorted all the cards in the personal values deck, it might look something like this:

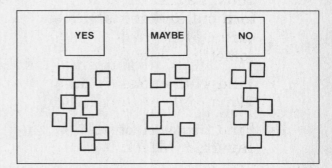

Step 4. Collect all of the personal values cards you placed under the YES card.

   a. Get the three cards that you set aside that say **Must have it, Nice to have it,** and **Can get along without it**. Lay them out as you did the YES, NO, and MAYBE cards.

   b. Look at your first YES card.

     ■ If you **need** this value in your life, put the card below the **Must have it** card.

     ■ If you **would like to have** this value in your life, put it under the **Nice to have it** card.

     ■ If you **don't need** it in your life, put it under the **Can get along without it** card.

Your card sort might look something like this:

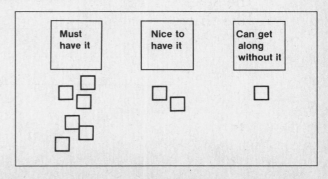

■ Values Summary

Now you will write a **summary**. A summary is a short statement or list of important information or ideas. In this case, the Values Summary is a list of the values that you have decided are most important to you.

Summary Directions

Step 1. Get the cards that you put under the **Must have it** card.

Step 2. Go through these cards. Think about how important each value is to you. Take your time and really think about each value.

Step 3. From these cards, choose your five most important **personal values**. List them below in Part 1—Personal Values.

Step 4. Now take the **Work Values** deck of cards. Follow the Card Sort Steps 1-4. Then, follow the Summary Steps 1-3.

Finally, repeat all of these steps with the **People Values** deck.

Part 1—Personal Values

1. _____

2. _____

3. _____

4. _____

5. _____

Part 2—Work Values

1. _____

2. _____

3. _____

4. _____

5. _____

Part 3—People Values

1. _____
2. _____
3. _____
4. _____
5. _____

Charting Your Career Path

Each activity that you do in this book leads you closer to a career choice. To help make this choice, you will copy what you've learned onto a chart on page 56.

■ Turn to the chart on page 56. Copy your five Personal Values from page 8 onto the chart. Look at the example below.

Job Family # _____ _____	MY VALUES	First Job Interest _____
Personal	1 Feel good about myself	◯
	2 Be happy	◯
	3 Be in charge of my own life	◯
	4 Have no worries about money	◯
	5 Have good health	◯
Work	1	◯

■ Copy your Work Values from page 8 onto the chart.

■ Now copy your five People Values from page 9 onto the chart.

■ Finally, copy the same information onto the second chart, on page 58.

What Have You Learned?

Look at the values you listed on the Values Summary (pages 8–9). You may have learned new things about yourself. You may have found that some values are more important to you than you knew. Maybe you found that certain values need to be part of your career.

Use the space below to show what you have learned about yourself in this unit. You may want to write or draw something. You can even cut words and pictures out of a magazine and paste them here.

SKILLS
UNIT TWO

 # What Are Your Best Skills?

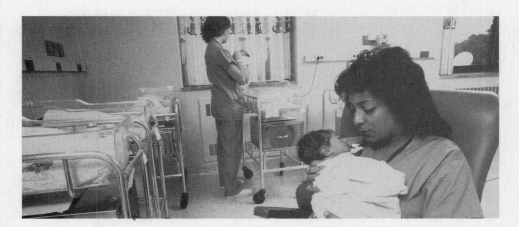

In Unit One, you learned about your values. In this unit, you will learn about your **skills**, abilities, and talents. Skills are things you can do well. Some of these, like welding, you learn on a job. Other skills you have, like working with others or following directions, are learned outside of work, but can be used at many jobs.

 ## How This Unit Will Help You

All jobs require skills. People are usually happy and successful when they use their best skills on the job. If you know what your best skills are, you can make good choices about jobs.

In this unit you will

■ learn what you are good at—your **everyday skills** and your **job skills**

■ decide which of your skills you **enjoy** using

■ write a **summary** of your skills

What Are Your Everyday Skills?

Everyday Skills are things you learned as you grew up and became an adult. These skills can include listening well, following directions, or working with other people. Many of these skills are needed on a job.

Directions

Step 1. Read the list of everyday skills below. Put a check (✓) by those things you **can do**.

☑ example

☐ sell things

☐ think of new ways to do things

☐ work with numbers

☐ figure out how things work

☐ think things through

☐ take risks

☐ know what something is worth

☐ get the information you need

☐ keep busy

☐ put ideas together

☐ teach others

☐ decide what to do next

☐ learn all about something

☐ make new things

☐ use tools

☐ put things together

☐ type letters

☐ work with money

☐ work carefully

☐ get things done

☐ use your time wisely

☐ be artistic

☐ tell the truth

☐ be counted on

☐ meet new people easily

☐ work well with others

☐ get others to do things

☐ follow directions

☐ listen carefully

☐ make things go smoothly

☐ take pride in what you do

☐ work quickly

☐ make changes if needed

☐ help others

☐ work well alone

☐ learn new things

☐ do more than one thing at a time

☐ put a lot of energy into a project

Step 2. Look only at the skills you have checked (✓).

Step 3. Put a second check by the things you are **very good** at doing.   ✓☑ example

Step 4. Look at only those skills that have two checks (✓☑).

Step 5. Of the skills with two checks, circle the **five** skills that you do **best**.   ⟨✓☑⟩example

Use the space below to write down the five skills you circled. These are your five **best** everyday skills.

1. _____

2. _____

3. _____

4. _____

5. _____

Charting Your Career Path

Each activity that you do in this book leads you closer to a career choice. To help make this choice, you will copy what you've learned onto a chart on page 56.

■ Turn to the chart on page 56. Copy your five best Everyday Skills onto the chart. Look at the example below.

How all of my VALUES match this Job Interest		◯
	MY SKILLS	
	1 *work carefully*	◯
Everyday	2 *learn all about something*	◯
	3 *work well alone*	◯
	4 *be counted on*	◯
	5 *think things through*	◯

■ Copy the same information onto the second chart, on page 58.

José's Story

José Morales was a welder. He worked hard every day, and the pay was good. But when he got home, he always went to the kitchen and began the work he *really* liked. Each night, he made eight to ten jars of salsa for family and friends. Everyone seemed to love it. Although it made a long day, José enjoyed the work. He especially liked choosing fresh ingredients and showing his family how to help.

One day, Mrs. Ellis at the corner market asked José to let her sell the salsa at her market. José was happy to do so. Soon, though, José found himself too busy to keep up. He could not be both a welder and a businessman. So, with the help of Mrs. Ellis—who loaned him the money to get started—José quit welding. He began to make salsa full time. José did not like to do any math, so he hired a bookkeeper to help.

Soon, his salsa was selling in many stores. José still worked long hours and did not earn as much as a welder. But he liked the work, and he liked to be his own boss.

Questions About the Story

1. What was José's hobby?

   _____

2. Using the everyday skills list on page 12, write in three skills you think José used in his hobby:

   a. _____

   b. _____

   c. _____

3. José decided to turn his hobby into a new career. What was his new career?

   _____

4. Do you have any hobbies? What are they?

   _____

   _____

5. What **everyday skills** do you use in your hobby?

   _____

   _____

6. How do you feel about using your everyday skills in a job or career?

   _____

   _____

   _____

   _____

_____

Answers

1. making salsa   2. answers will vary   3. making and selling salsa
4., 5., and 6. answers will vary

What Job Skills Do You Have?

On page 13, you listed your five best **everyday skills**.
Now you are ready to learn about your **job skills**. These
are the skills used in certain jobs. Some job skills—like
using a special tool—are used only in certain jobs. Many
job skills—like following directions and speaking
clearly—are used in many different jobs.

People are usually happiest in jobs that fit their skills
and their style. For example, very friendly people may like
social jobs where they can talk to others. People with
artistic skill may like jobs where they can be creative.

"Social" and "artistic" are two types of **job families**—
groups of jobs that require the same type of skills. Each
job family requires certain skills and fits a certain style.
If you have many skills in a job family, then that job
family might fit you best. Of course, no job family is a
perfect fit for one person. You may see that you fit into all
six groups!

Career counselors often use the names of these job
families. It may help you to know the names, but don't
worry about trying to remember them. The six pictures on
the opposite page each stand for a certain job family.

Job skills are grouped into **job families**, or types of jobs. The six groups of job families were created by John Holland in the *Self-Directed Search*. The six job families are:

Realistic:
People in these jobs like to work outdoors and use tools and machines. They enjoy making things with their hands. Some jobs they may like are mechanic, construction worker, or fish and wildlife worker.

Investigative:
This group likes to solve problems, know about things, and stay with something until it is finished. They may want to work alone. Some jobs they may like are pharmacist, food tester, or tax preparer.

Artistic:
People in this group like to be creative or entertaining. They may want to work alone, and they often come up with something new and different. Some jobs they may like are photographer, singer, or disk jockey.

Social:
This group cares about other people. They like to help others solve problems. They do not like to work with machines or do the same work every day. Some jobs they may like are teacher, counselor, or probation officer.

Enterprising:
People in these jobs can sell things and lead others. They have energy and confidence. They do not like to do detailed work or take a long time to solve problems. Jobs they may like are flight attendant, real estate agent, or sports promoter.

Conventional:
These people want to know exactly what they should do on the job. They fit well in a big company, but they do not want to be the boss. They are usually very dependable and like the business world. Some jobs they may like are bank teller, mail carrier, or secretary.

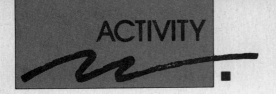

 # What Are Your Best Job Skills?

This activity will help you explore your **job skills**. When you finish, you will know which job skills you have, and which you like to use. You will know which **job families** may fit your style.

Each page in this activity has lists of job skills for each job family. The job family title is at the top of the page.

Directions

Step 1. Look at page 20, the Realistic job skills. Notice the two headings, My Mechanical Skills and My Nature Skills. Under each heading is a list of job skills. For each skill, put a check in the YES or MAYBE box. Read each skill and check

- **YES** if you have ever used this skill, on or off a job

YES	MAYBE
☑	☐

- **MAYBE** if you have never used this skill, but you think you could use it

YES	MAYBE
☐	☑

If you do **not** think you can use a skill, do not check it. Go with your first reaction.

For example, your My Nature Skills may look something like this:

> **My Nature Skills**
>
> | | YES | MAYBE |
> |---|-----|-------|
> | feed and water animals | ☑ | ☐ |
> | trim hedges | ☑ | ☐ |
> | put fertilizer on lawns | ☐ | ☑ |
> | plant grass and flowers | ☐ | ☑ |
> | bathe animals | ☐ | ☐ |

Step 2. Once you have checked YES or MAYBE, think about whether you would like to use this job skill. **Circle** the skills you would **enjoy** using on a job.

- This shows that you have used the skill, and **would enjoy** using it on a job.

YES	MAYBE
	☐

■ This shows that you have never used the skill, but you think you **might enjoy** using it on a job.

YES MAYBE
□ ☑ (circled)

There may be items that you did **not** circle. These are the skills that you do not enjoy. For example, you may be a very good cook. But, because you had to cook meals for your large family most of your life, you don't enjoy using this skill now.

■ Not circling a skill, even a skill checked YES, means you would **not** enjoy using it on a job.

YES MAYBE
☑ □

When you have finished this activity, your My Nature Skills list may look something like this:

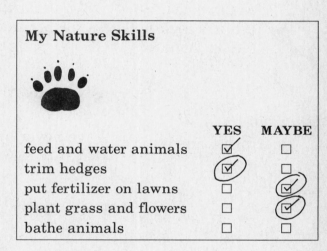

My Nature Skills

	YES	MAYBE
feed and water animals	☑	□
trim hedges	☑ (circled)	□
put fertilizer on lawns	□	☑ (circled)
plant grass and flowers	□	☑ (circled)
bathe animals	□	□

Step 3. As you finish each job family, count up the number of skills that you **circled**. Put this number in the Job Skills Tally box at the bottom of the page. This will help you see which job families may best fit your skills.

Your tally box might look like this:

Job Skills Tally

Number of job skills you **enjoy** in the **Realistic** job family:

_3_

Step 4. Go through each list on pages 20–29. Check YES or MAYBE for each skill. **Circle** the skills you **enjoy** using. Then, **count** your circled skills and put the number in the tally box.

 **Realistic**

- Check YES or MAYBE for each skill.
- Circle the skills you enjoy.
- Count your circled skills and put the number in the tally box.

My Mechanical Skills

	YES	MAYBE
use hand tools	☐	☐
find car problems	☐	☐
change parts	☐	☐
use math	☐	☐
read directions	☐	☐
read dials and meters	☐	☐
drive a car	☐	☐
put things together	☐	☐
fix a TV or radio	☐	☐
build things	☐	☐
measure things	☐	☐

My Nature Skills

	YES	MAYBE
feed and water animals	☐	☐
trim hedges	☐	☐
put fertilizer on lawns	☐	☐
plant grass and flowers	☐	☐
bathe animals	☐	☐
mow lawns	☐	☐
build trails	☐	☐

My Construction Skills

	YES	MAYBE
work with my hands	☐	☐
use hand tools	☐	☐
use power tools	☐	☐
use math to measure	☐	☐
do exact work	☐	☐
work safely	☐	☐
follow directions	☐	☐
see what to do next	☐	☐

My Driving Skills

	YES	MAYBE
follow directions	☐	☐
obey traffic rules	☐	☐
keep records	☐	☐
drive a car	☐	☐
drive a truck	☐	☐
be on time	☐	☐
work with others	☐	☐
handle money	☐	☐
read maps	☐	☐

Job Skills Tally

Number of job skills you **enjoy** in the **Realistic** job family:

_____

 Investigative

- Check YES or MAYBE for each skill.
- Circle the skills you enjoy.
- Count your circled skills and put the number in the tally box.

My Medical Service Skills

	YES	MAYBE
work with people	☐	☐
follow exact directions	☐	☐
listen carefully	☐	☐
use special machines	☐	☐
write reports	☐	☐
work under stress	☐	☐
work odd hours	☐	☐
remember details	☐	☐
see small differences	☐	☐
care for others	☐	☐

My Medical Science Skills

	YES	MAYBE
follow rules exactly	☐	☐
use lab equipment	☐	☐
solve problems	☐	☐
read scientific papers	☐	☐
mix formulas	☐	☐
notice small differences	☐	☐
write reports	☐	☐

My Math Skills

	YES	MAYBE
keep books	☐	☐
figure costs	☐	☐
make scale drawings	☐	☐
use geometry	☐	☐
read dials and meters	☐	☐
measure things	☐	☐
check for errors	☐	☐
solve number problems	☐	☐

My Science Skills

	YES	MAYBE
spot trouble	☐	☐
read handbooks	☐	☐
use tools that measure	☐	☐
use small hand tools	☐	☐
use math	☐	☐
ask questions	☐	☐
see how things fit together	☐	☐

Job Skills Tally

Number of job skills you **enjoy** in the **Investigative** job family:

____

 Artistic

- Check YES or MAYBE for each skill.
- Circle the skills you enjoy.
- Count your circled skills and put the number in the tally box.

My Musical Skills

	YES	MAYBE
sing	☐	☐
read music	☐	☐
use music theory	☐	☐
hear differences in musical tones	☐	☐
play a musical instrument	☐	☐
learn pieces of music	☐	☐
follow exact directions	☐	☐
listen carefully	☐	☐
help others learn	☐	☐

My Drama Skills

	YES	MAYBE
act a part in a play	☐	☐
learn a script	☐	☐
speak clearly	☐	☐
tell stories with my voice or body	☐	☐
follow exact directions	☐	☐
be confident	☐	☐
make people laugh	☐	☐
talk or sing in front of a group	☐	☐

My Art Skills

	YES	MAYBE
use math	☐	☐
use camera equipment	☐	☐
use lighting equipment	☐	☐
follow directions	☐	☐
work under pressure	☐	☐
sell my work	☐	☐
use art to show feelings, thoughts, and ideas	☐	☐
draw	☐	☐
paint	☐	☐
sculpt	☐	☐

My Communication Skills

	YES	MAYBE
write clearly	☐	☐
speak clearly	☐	☐
sell ideas or products	☐	☐
gather information	☐	☐
type	☐	☐
work under pressure	☐	☐
meet deadlines	☐	☐
listen well	☐	☐
work well with people	☐	☐
speak more than one language	☐	☐

Job Skills Tally

Number of job skills you **enjoy** in the **Artistic** job family:

____

Social

- Check YES or MAYBE for each skill.
- Circle the skills you enjoy.
- Count your circled skills and put the number in the tally box.

My Teaching Skills

	YES	MAYBE
listen well	☐	☐
explain things clearly	☐	☐
remember details	☐	☐
share ideas with others	☐	☐
use math	☐	☐
talk in front of groups	☐	☐
help others	☐	☐
learn and use facts	☐	☐
be exact in my work	☐	☐
find small differences in words and numbers	☐	☐

My Athletic Skills

	YES	MAYBE
lead or teach games	☐	☐
help people stay fit	☐	☐
lift weights	☐	☐
be a good team member	☐	☐
coach team sports	☐	☐
keep records	☐	☐
understand sports	☐	☐

My Social Service Skills

	YES	MAYBE
meet people easily	☐	☐
keep records	☐	☐
plan my day's work	☐	☐
listen well	☐	☐
explain things clearly	☐	☐
be patient	☐	☐
read technical information	☐	☐
help people solve problems	☐	☐
use community resources	☐	☐

My Domestic Arts Skills

	YES	MAYBE
work well with people	☐	☐
clean a house	☐	☐
do laundry	☐	☐
cook meals	☐	☐
shop for food	☐	☐
keep records	☐	☐
plan my time well	☐	☐
follow directions	☐	☐

Job Skills Tally

Number of job skills you **enjoy** in the **Social** job family:

———

Enterprising

- Check YES or MAYBE for each skill.
- Circle the skills you enjoy.
- Count your circled skills and put the number in the tally box.

My Sales Skills

	YES	MAYBE
use math	☐	☐
handle money	☐	☐
work with people	☐	☐
write reports of sales	☐	☐
take and fill orders	☐	☐
keep track of goods	☐	☐
drive a car	☐	☐
work under pressure	☐	☐
follow directions	☐	☐
operate basic business machines	☐	☐

My Service Skills

	YES	MAYBE
work with people	☐	☐
keep books and records	☐	☐
order supplies	☐	☐
work under pressure	☐	☐
give personal care	☐	☐
speak clearly	☐	☐
know what customers want	☐	☐
work odd hours	☐	☐

Job Skills Tally

Number of job skills you **enjoy** in the **Enterprising** job family:

___

Conventional

- Check YES or MAYBE for each skill.
- Circle the skills you enjoy.
- Count your circled skills and put the number in the tally box.

My Office Skills

	YES	MAYBE
type	☐	☐
take dictation	☐	☐
spell correctly	☐	☐
follow directions	☐	☐
work with others	☐	☐
take phone messages	☐	☐
file information	☐	☐
keep records	☐	☐
prepare bank deposits	☐	☐
use math	☐	☐
use office machines	☐	☐
get and use confidential information	☐	☐

My Production and Assembly Skills

	YES	MAYBE
follow directions exactly	☐	☐
put parts together	☐	☐
work quickly	☐	☐
read dials and meters	☐	☐
read drawings	☐	☐
check work for quality	☐	☐
notice small details	☐	☐
use chemicals safely	☐	☐
use special tools and machines	☐	☐

Job Skills Tally

Number of job skills you **enjoy** in the **Conventional** job family:

———

 # Job Skills Summary

Congratulations! You have finished the job skills activity. You have found the skills you have used, and the skills that you might enjoy using on a job.

Now you will decide which job families best fit your skills and your style.

Directions

Step 1. Look at the Job Skills Tally boxes on pages 21–29. Below, write the number of job skills you **enjoy** in each job family.

Job Family	Number of Job Skills You Enjoy
Realistic	_____
Investigative	_____
Artistic	_____
Social	_____
Enterprising	_____
Conventional	_____

Step 2. Which **two** job families above have the most skills you enjoy? These two job families may fit you best. Draw a star (✗) by these top two job families. Draw a star (✗) by these same two job families on page 31.

Step 3. Look back at the skills lists on pages 20–29 for these two job families. Copy your **circled** YES skills under the two job families that you starred (✗) on page 31.

If you prefer, you may write your **circled** YES skills for all six job families. Write in the margins if you need to.

Step 4. Finally, go back through the skills you listed on page 31. **Circle** your four best skills in each job family. These are the skills that you do best and that you enjoy doing.

REALISTIC   YES ☑

_____

_____

_____

_____

INVESTIGATIVE   YES ☑

_____

_____

_____

_____

ARTISTIC   YES ☑

_____

_____

_____

_____

SOCIAL   YES ☑

_____

_____

_____

_____

ENTERPRISING   YES ☑

_____

_____

_____

_____

CONVENTIONAL   YES ☑

_____

_____

_____

_____

Charting Your Career Path

Each activity that you do in this book leads you closer to a career choice. To help make this choice, you will copy what you've learned onto a chart on page 56.

■ Turn to the chart on page 56.

■ Copy the name of the first job family that you starred (✶) on page 31 onto the top of the chart on page 56. Look at the example below.

✶INVESTIGATIVE YES ☑

(follow exact directions) _____ (use lab equipment) _____

write reports _____ measure things _____

(remember details) _____ see how things fit together _____

(see small differences) _____ _____

Job Family # _____	MY VALUES		First Job Interest
→ _Investigative_			_____
Personal	1		◯
	2		◯

■ Find your four best job skills for that same job family. These will be the four YES skills that you circled on page 31. Copy these four skills onto the chart. Here is an example.

		First Job Interest
Job	1 follow exact directions	◯
	2 remember details	◯
	3 see small differences	◯
	4 use lab equipment	◯

■ Find the second job family that you starred (✶) on page 31. Copy the name of this job family onto the top of the chart on page 58.

■ Now copy your four best job skills from that same job family onto the chart on page 58.

Job Skills History

Look at page 31. You circled your best skills in at least two job families. Choose any two of these circled skills and write them below. Describe when and where you used these skills. How did they help you to be successful on a project or activity?

Skill: _____

When and where did you use this skill? How did it help you to be successful on a project or activity?

_____

_____

_____

_____

Skill: _____

When and where did you use this skill? How did it help you to be successful on a project or activity?

_____

_____

_____

_____

Look back through pages 20–29. Did you circle any MAYBE skills? How would you use these skills someday? Write your thoughts about using one of these skills in the future.

_____

_____

_____

_____

What Have You Learned?

You have done a lot of hard work. You now know your best everyday skills and your favorite job skills. Knowing about these skills will help you decide which career will fit you best.

Use the space below to show what you learned about yourself in this unit. You may want to write or draw something. You can even cut words and pictures out of a magazine and paste them here.

What Jobs Interest You?

You have thought about your values and about the skills you have or want to have. Now you are ready to take the next step toward your career path. In this unit, you will look into your **job interests**.

Your job interests are those jobs that you may want to learn more about. A job may interest you because the title sounds good. Maybe someone you know has a job you think you might like. For whatever reason, a job interest is a job that you want to look into.

How This Unit Will Help You

A job that is interesting to you is one that you are likely to keep. If you meet your job interests, you will be likely to enjoy your job.

In this unit you will

■ learn about **job interests**

■ decide about your own **job interests**

■ **summarize** your choices

■ think about what your **job interests** might mean

Anna's Story

Anna Ivanova was very proud of herself. Only three years ago, she had left Russia and come to this country. Already, thanks to the classes she took, Anna had learned English. Anna's younger sister Katrina lived with her. Anna worked nights at a bakery to support them both.

Anna wanted to change jobs. In Moscow, she had worked for many years as a clerk at a state store. She did not like the job, and she did not want to do it again. In her English class, she talked to her teacher about getting a new job. Her teacher sent her to the career counseling office.

Ms. Díaz, the career counselor, gave Anna a long list of job titles to look at. This list was called a job interest inventory. Jobs were listed under six job families. Anna was surprised to see so many jobs. She knew what many of the jobs were about. There were some jobs, however, that Anna had never heard of.

Anna read each job title and checked YES or MAYBE beside it. If a job sounded good to her, she checked YES next to the job title.

She also checked MAYBE by many jobs. These were jobs she did not know about, but thought she might like to learn about.

When Anna finished the job interest inventory, she was glad. She was ready to talk with Ms. Díaz. She wanted to know what her job choices meant.

Thinking About Anna's Choices

Anna met with Ms. Díaz. They looked at her choices on the inventory. They wanted to find the job families that had the **most interesting** jobs for her.

The counselor asked Anna to imagine a **thermometer** that measured her feelings about jobs. She knew that a thermometer measured hot and cold. Ms. Díaz said that job families with **many** YES and MAYBE checks are HOT. They have the most interesting jobs. Job families with very **few** YES and MAYBE checks are COLD. They may not have any interesting jobs.

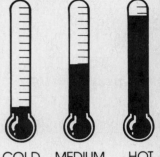

COLD   MEDIUM   HOT

Anna had checked YES and MAYBE by *many* jobs in both the Social and Investigative job families. She knew that these were her HOT job families.

Anna had a few YES and MAYBE checks under Artistic, Enterprising, and Conventional. These jobs were in the middle of the thermometer. But, she had not checked any job title under Realistic. She knew that she was not interested in these jobs.

1. One of Anna's HOT job families was the Social job family. Shade this thermometer to show Anna's feelings about this job family.

2. One of Anna's MEDIUM job families was the Artistic job family. Shade the thermometer to show Anna's feelings about this job family.

Questions About Anna's Job Interests

1. What other job family, besides Social, is a HOT one for Anna?

_____

2. What job family was a COLD one for Anna?

_____

3. Anna has found two job families she likes. What might be the next step for Anna to take?

_____

_____

_____

▪ JUST FOR **FUN** ▪

Each word in the list below can be found in the puzzle.
Look across, down, and diagonally to find words. Try to
find at least five words. When you find a word, circle it in
the puzzle and mark it off the list.

Words

RISK	LEARN	TIME
INFORM	MAKE	SKILLS
MONEY	LISTEN	~~JOB~~
IDEAS	TEACH	PEOPLE
NUMBERS	HELP	CAREER
THINK	CAREFUL	

```
I   D   E   A   S   S   K   I   L   L   S
Q   N   N   Z   L   I   S   T   E   N   V
P   X   F   M   E   M   T   H   I   N   K
G   W   N   O   A   C   A   R   E   E   R
J   H   U   N   R   I   S   K   D   T   X
K   O   M   E   N   M   B   Z   E   I   Y
K   Z   B   Y   T   E   A   C   H   M   T
V   P   E   O   P   L   E   Z   E   E   Y
C   A   R   E   F   U   L   X   L   Q   R
Y   T   S   B   H   G   V   W   P   L   A
```

 # What Jobs Sound Good to You?

Finding out about your job interests is an important step in choosing a career. You will take a **job interest inventory** like the one Anna took. This activity will help you decide what jobs may fit you best.

Directions

Step 1. On page 30, you drew a star (★) by the **two** job families that best fit your skills. Now, draw a star by those same job families below.

Step 2. Pages 42–47 have lists of jobs for each job family. Some jobs will sound more interesting than others. Turn to the first page that you starred (★) above. Read each job title and check

	YES	MAYBE
■ **YES** if the job sounds good to you	☑	☐
■ **MAYBE** if a job sounds OK, but you need to find out more about it	☐	☑

If a job does **not** sound good to you, do not check it.

Work fast, and go with your first feeling about each job. That first feeling is often closest to the truth.

Step 3. When you finish each page that you starred (★), shade in the thermometer for that page. This will show how many YES and MAYBE checks you have in that job family.

Step 4. Finally, write a summary like the one shown here. List the YES or MAYBE jobs that interest you **most**. List up to seven jobs. Start with your YES jobs.

For example, your Conventional job family may look like this:

Conventional

List up to 7 jobs that interest you **most**.

<u>Mail carrier</u>

<u>Messenger</u>

<u>Mail clerk</u>

<u>Quality control clerk</u>

<u>Bank teller</u>

<u>Small products assembler</u>

You may want to go through each page in the job interest inventory, not just the **two** pages that you starred (★). This will help you check your job interests in many different areas.

Realistic

- Check YES or MAYBE.
- Shade in the thermometer.
- List up to seven jobs that interest you most.

Mechanical Jobs	YES	MAYBE
television repairer	☐	☐
auto mechanic	☐	☐
small engine repairer	☐	☐
appliance repairer	☐	☐
upholstery worker	☐	☐
tire repairer	☐	☐
printing press operator	☐	☐
service station attendant	☐	☐
shoe repairer	☐	☐
laundry or dry cleaning worker	☐	☐
optician	☐	☐
auto body repairer	☐	☐
computer repairer	☐	☐
plastic machine operator	☐	☐
broadcast technician	☐	☐
water and waste water treatment operator	☐	☐

Construction Jobs	YES	MAYBE
tile setter	☐	☐
painter	☐	☐
carpenter	☐	☐
bricklayer	☐	☐
electrician	☐	☐
helper or laborer	☐	☐

Nature Jobs	YES	MAYBE
floral designer	☐	☐
farm worker	☐	☐
dog groomer	☐	☐
groundskeeper	☐	☐
survey helper	☐	☐
animal caretaker	☐	☐
forester aide	☐	☐
gardener	☐	☐
nursery worker	☐	☐

Driving Jobs	YES	MAYBE
truck driver	☐	☐
heavy equipment operator	☐	☐
bus driver	☐	☐
taxi driver	☐	☐
limo driver	☐	☐

Realistic

List up to 7 jobs that interest you **most**.

_____

_____

_____

_____

_____

_____

_____

Investigative

- ■ Check YES or MAYBE.
- ■ Shade in the thermometer.
- ■ List up to seven jobs that interest you most.

Medical Service Jobs

	YES	MAYBE
respiratory therapist	☐	☐
nursing aide	☐	☐
physician assistant	☐	☐
licensed practical nurse	☐	☐
medical assistant	☐	☐
physical therapy aide	☐	☐
dental assistant	☐	☐

Medical Science Jobs

	YES	MAYBE
radiologic technician	☐	☐
medical records clerk	☐	☐
laboratory technician	☐	☐
pharmacy assistant	☐	☐
research assistant	☐	☐
eyeglass lab technician	☐	☐

Math Jobs

	YES	MAYBE
tax preparer	☐	☐
electrical tester	☐	☐

Science Jobs

	YES	MAYBE
laboratory assistant	☐	☐
drafter	☐	☐
chemical engineer	☐	☐
food tester	☐	☐
scientific helper	☐	☐
dietitian	☐	☐

Investigative

List up to 7 jobs that interest you **most**.

_____

_____

_____

_____

_____

_____

_____

Artistic

- Check YES or MAYBE.
- Shade in the thermometer.
- List up to seven jobs that interest you most.

Musical Jobs	YES	MAYBE
singer	☐	☐
band director	☐	☐
choral director	☐	☐
instrument player	☐	☐
composer	☐	☐
music teacher	☐	☐
arranger	☐	☐

Drama Jobs	YES	MAYBE
actor/actress	☐	☐
drama teacher	☐	☐
dancer	☐	☐
clown	☐	☐
director	☐	☐
disk jockey	☐	☐

Art Jobs	YES	MAYBE
visual artist	☐	☐
photographer	☐	☐
sketch artist	☐	☐
graphic artist	☐	☐
makeup artist	☐	☐
greeting card designer	☐	☐
painting instructor	☐	☐
sculptor	☐	☐

Communications Jobs	YES	MAYBE
writer	☐	☐
editor	☐	☐
reporter	☐	☐
advertising aide	☐	☐
fundraiser	☐	☐
lobbyist	☐	☐
public relations worker	☐	☐
radio announcer	☐	☐
TV announcer	☐	☐

Artistic

List up to 7 jobs that interest you **most**.

_____

_____

_____

_____

_____

_____

_____

Social

- Check YES or MAYBE.
- Shade in the thermometer.
- List up to seven jobs that interest you most.

Teaching Jobs	YES	MAYBE
employment interviewer	☐	☐
elementary teacher	☐	☐
library assistant	☐	☐
nursery school attendant	☐	☐
preschool teacher	☐	☐
teacher aide	☐	☐

Athletic Jobs	YES	MAYBE
playground leader	☐	☐
lifeguard	☐	☐
health spa attendant	☐	☐
fitness club worker	☐	☐
camp counselor	☐	☐
activities leader	☐	☐
recreation assistant	☐	☐

Social Service Jobs	YES	MAYBE
caseworker	☐	☐
case aide	☐	☐
counselor	☐	☐
paralegal	☐	☐
police officer	☐	☐
passenger service representative	☐	☐

Domestic Arts Jobs	YES	MAYBE
home health aide	☐	☐
nursing home aide	☐	☐
adult daycare aide	☐	☐
companion	☐	☐
hospital orderly	☐	☐
private household worker	☐	☐

Social

List up to 7 jobs that interest you **most**.

_____

_____

_____

_____

_____

_____

_____

Enterprising

- Check YES or MAYBE.
- Shade in the thermometer.
- List up to seven jobs that interest you most.

Sales Jobs	YES	MAYBE
counter clerk	☐	☐
insurance salesperson	☐	☐
bank teller	☐	☐
retail sales worker	☐	☐
postal clerk	☐	☐
real estate agent	☐	☐
sales route driver	☐	☐
manufacturer's sales representative	☐	☐

Service Jobs	YES	MAYBE
barber	☐	☐
flight attendant	☐	☐
cosmetologist	☐	☐
caretaker	☐	☐
host or hostess	☐	☐
cafeteria worker	☐	☐
janitor	☐	☐
travel agent	☐	☐
hotel or motel clerk	☐	☐

Enterprising

List up to 7 jobs that interest you **most**.

_____

_____

_____

_____

_____

_____

_____

Conventional

- Check YES or MAYBE.
- Shade in the thermometer.
- List up to seven jobs that interest you most.

Office Jobs	YES	MAYBE
credit clerk	☐	☐
data entry keyer	☐	☐
receptionist	☐	☐
order taker	☐	☐
file clerk	☐	☐
billing clerk	☐	☐
secretary	☐	☐
office worker	☐	☐
computer operator	☐	☐
bank teller	☐	☐
posting clerk	☐	☐
word processing operator	☐	☐

Production and Assembly Jobs	YES	MAYBE
sewing machine operator	☐	☐
food or grocery checker	☐	☐
stock clerk	☐	☐
baker	☐	☐
small parts assembler	☐	☐
small products assembler	☐	☐
quality control clerk	☐	☐
mail clerk	☐	☐
mail carrier	☐	☐
messenger	☐	☐

Conventional

List up to 7 jobs that interest you **most**.

_____

_____

_____

_____

_____

_____

_____

 # Rating Your Job Interests

Now that you have finished your job interest inventory, you have from two to six lists of jobs. The jobs you listed sound good to you, or might sound good if you knew more about them.

In this activity, you will decide which job family has the jobs you are **most interested** in. It will be called **Job Family #1**.

Directions

Step 1. Look over your job interest inventory on pages 42–47. You shaded in at least two thermometers. The thermometers show how you feel about each job family.

Find the thermometer that you shaded in **most**. It may look something like the one to the right.

This is the job family that you are most interested in. We will call it Job Family #1.

Step 2. Cut out the list of your most interesting jobs for that job family. Paste or tape it onto page 49. Place it in the top space for Job Family #1. If you prefer, you may write your list in the space given.

Step 3. After you have pasted or written in Job Family #1, repeat Steps 1 and 2 above to find your second best job family, Job Family #2.

Use this space to tape, paste, or write your lists of the most interesting jobs. These lists show which two job families have the best jobs for you.

Job Family #1
The job family that you think has the most interesting jobs goes in this box. Paste, tape, or write the job list here.

Job Family #2
The job family that you think has the next most interesting jobs goes in this box. Paste, tape, or write the job list here.

Deciding on Your Job Interests

To decide about the jobs that fit you best, you may need more information. On page 65, you will find the Jobs Glossary. A **glossary** is a list of special words and their meanings. To learn more about the jobs that interest you, look for the job titles in the Jobs Glossary.

Directions

Step 1. Look at the list on page 49 for Job Family #1. Decide which job interests you **most**. Mark it with a 1. Then choose the second and third most interesting jobs. Mark them 2 and 3.

Step 2. Follow the same steps for Job Family #2.

Step 3. Now write your first, second, and third job choices for each job family below.

Job Family #1: _____

first: _____ second: _____ third: _____

Why do these jobs sound good to you? Write your answer below.

_____

_____

Job Family #2: _____

first: _____ second: _____ third: _____

Why do these jobs sound good to you? Write your answer below.

_____

_____

Charting Your Career Path

■ Turn to the chart on page 56. Look at the job family title that you wrote at the top of the chart. Is this job family one of the two families you listed on page 50?

 ■ If it **is**, then mark it **#1** or **#2**, just as it is on page 50. Then copy your first, second, and third Job Interest for that job family onto the chart. Look at the example below.

 ■ If it is **not**, then ask your teacher for a clean copy of the chart. You will need to look at your job skills for this job family. Your teacher can help you do this.

Job Family #1 _Investigative_	MY VALUES	First Job Interest _research assistant_	Second Job Interest _lab technician_	Third Job Interest _medical records clerk_
Personal	1			
	2			

■ Now turn to the chart on page 58. Look at the job family title that you wrote at the top of the chart. Is this job family one of the two families you listed on page 50?

 ■ If it **is**, then mark it #1 or #2, just as it is on page 50. Then, copy your first, second, and third Job Interest for that job family onto the chart.

 ■ If it is **not**, ask your teacher for help.

What Have You Learned?

Congratulations! You have made many discoveries about your job interests. Look over page 50, Deciding on Your Job Interests. You may wish to talk this over with someone. What did you learn? Were there any surprises? What steps do you think you need to take now? Use this page to write or draw your thoughts.

CAREERS
UNIT FOUR

What Is on Your Career Path?

In this last unit, you will compare your job interests with your values and your skills. You will end up with a few jobs that you may want to find out more about. These jobs may fit into your **career path**.

You will also think about your **barriers** and **strengths**. Barriers might stop you from reaching your goals. Strengths will help you move around barriers to reach your goals.

 ## How This Unit Will Help You

Your values, skills, and interests all work together. When you find a job that meets all three, you may be more successful.

In this unit you will

■ compare your **job interests** with your **values** and **skills**

■ find a few **jobs** that may fit you

■ look at your **barriers** and your **strengths**

 # Which Jobs Fit You Best?

Each activity that you have done in this book has led you closer to a career choice. Now you will finish the charts you have been working on. You will see how well your values and skills match your job interests. You will find a few jobs that may fit your career path.

You may need more information about a job. If so, look the job up in the Jobs Glossary at the end of the book.

Directions
Look at the chart you marked Job Family #1 (page 56 or 58). It should be nearly complete!

Step 1. Matching Values

Look at your First Job Interest. Think about how much your five Personal Values match this job. Ask yourself, "Does this job match this value?"

If the value matches the job

- **a lot**, shade the circle like this

- **somewhat**, but not a lot, shade the circle like this

- **not at all**, do not shade the circle

Shade all five circles next to your Personal Values. Then, repeat Step 1 for your Work Values and People Values. Look at this example.

The more fully a circle is shaded, the closer the match between this value and this job.

Job Family _#1_ _Investigative_	MY VALUES	First Job Interest _research assistant_
Personal	1 _Feel good about myself_	●
	2 _Be happy_	●
	3 _Be in charge of my own life_	◐
	4 _Have no worries about money_	◐
	5 _Have good health_	◐

Step 2. How You Feel About the Match

You have looked at 15 of your most important values. You have thought about how each value matches the job. Find the one large circle under the 15 small circles. Shade it in to show how you feel about the match between **all 15** of your values and this job interest.

If your values match this job interest a lot, you might shade the large circle like this.

Step 3. Matching Everyday Skills

Now look at your five Everyday Skills. Shade the circles as you did in Step 1. Ask yourself, "How much is this skill used on this job?"

Step 4. Matching Job Skills

Ask yourself, "How much is this skill used on this job?" Fill in the small circles to show the match between your job skills and this job.

Next, shade in the large circle under all nine of your skills. This will show how **all nine** of your skills match this job interest.

Step 5. Repeat Steps 1–4 for your Second Job Interest, then your Third Job Interest for Job Family #1.

Step 6. When the chart for Job Family #1 is all filled in, do the Summary at the right of the chart.

When you have finished Steps 1–6, repeat all of the steps for Job Family #2. Remember, this will help you find jobs that may fit into your career path!

Job Family #_____ _____	MY VALUES	First Job Interest _____
Personal	1	◯
	2	◯
	3	◯
	4	◯
	5	◯
Work	1	◯
	2	◯
	3	◯
	4	◯
	5	◯
People	1	◯
	2	◯
	3	◯
	4	◯
	5	◯
How all of my VALUES match this Job Interest		◯
	MY SKILLS	
Everyday	1	◯
	2	◯
	3	◯
	4	◯
	5	◯
Job	1	◯
	2	◯
	3	◯
	4	◯
How all of my SKILLS match this Job Interest		◯

Second Job Interest	Third Job Interest
1 ○	○
2 ○	○
3 ○	○
4 ○	○
5 ○	○
1 ○	○
2 ○	○
3 ○	○
4 ○	○
5 ○	○
1 ○	○
2 ○	○
3 ○	○
4 ○	○
5 ○	○
○	○
1 ○	○
2 ○	○
3 ○	○
4 ○	○
5 ○	○
1 ○	○
2 ○	○
3 ○	○
4 ○	○
○	○

Summary

You now know how each of your Job Interests matches your skills and values.

If a job matches **both** your skills and values, it may be a good career for you to learn more about.

Skills

Values

A good match

Write your First Job Interest:

_____

Shade the thermometer to show whether this job is a good match.

Write your Second Job Interest:

_____

Shade the thermometer to show whether this job is a good match.

Write your Third Job Interest:

_____

Shade the thermometer to show whether this job is a good match.

Are you willing to spend time and energy learning more about any of these jobs as a career?

If YES, list the job or jobs below.

_____

_____

_____

Job Family #_____ _____	MY VALUES	First Job Interest _____
Personal	1	◯
	2	◯
	3	◯
	4	◯
	5	◯
Work	1	◯
	2	◯
	3	◯
	4	◯
	5	◯
People	1	◯
	2	◯
	3	◯
	4	◯
	5	◯
How all of my VALUES match this Job Interest		◯
	MY SKILLS	
Everyday	1	◯
	2	◯
	3	◯
	4	◯
	5	◯
Job	1	◯
	2	◯
	3	◯
	4	◯
How all of my SKILLS match this Job Interest		◯

Second Job Interest	Third Job Interest
1 ◯	◯
2 ◯	◯
3 ◯	◯
4 ◯	◯
5 ◯	◯
1 ◯	◯
2 ◯	◯
3 ◯	◯
4 ◯	◯
5 ◯	◯
1 ◯	◯
2 ◯	◯
3 ◯	◯
4 ◯	◯
5 ◯	◯
◯	◯
1 ◯	◯
2 ◯	◯
3 ◯	◯
4 ◯	◯
5 ◯	◯
1 ◯	◯
2 ◯	◯
3 ◯	◯
4 ◯	◯
◯	◯

 # Summary

You now know how each of your Job Interests matches your skills and values.

If a job matches **both** your skills and values, it may be a good career for you to learn more about.

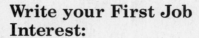

Write your First Job Interest:

_____

Shade the thermometer to show whether this job is a good match.

Write your Second Job Interest:

_____

Shade the thermometer to show whether this job is a good match.

Write your Third Job Interest:

_____

Shade the thermometer to show whether this job is a good match.

Are you willing to spend time and energy learning more about any of these jobs as a career?

If YES, list the job or jobs below.

_____

_____

_____

Barriers and Strengths

You have now made some decisions about some jobs that you want to learn more about. The next step is to look at your **barriers** and **strengths**.

 ## Barriers

Barriers are things that get in the way of something you want to do. They can act as walls that stand in front of you.

Some of these walls are inside you. These are things you tell yourself. Thoughts like "I am too old to change" or "I don't have enough money" are feelings you may have that keep you from changing.

Other barriers are outside of you. Facts about a job may be a wall that might stop you. For example, becoming a medical records clerk may require more training than you now have. How do you get the needed training? Or, you may find that jobs you want to learn about might require you to move to a new town. Can you and your family do that?

 ## Strengths

You also have strengths that will help you with these barriers. Strengths are things such as a good attitude, family support, and past successes. For example, you may know that you like to learn new things and that you are a hard worker. These are strengths that you can use to overcome barriers.

You need to consider both barriers and strengths as you chart your career path.

◰ Marvin's Story

"It really is hard to fit it together," Marvin Washington thought. First a values inventory, then a skills inventory. Then he had to find out about his job interests. It was a lot to do. Out of all this he had come up with four jobs he wanted to learn more about.

But how could he do any of these jobs? For example, what about being a truck driver? Wasn't he too old for this? Marvin also thought he would have trouble getting the money for training. He had to work and to support his family. How would he get the time? Between his job, family, and friends he barely had any time now.

He was talking with a friend in his adult education class. "I really want to do this, but I don't think I'm going to get a chance. It's like there is a big brick wall in front of me, and I can't get around it," Marvin said to his friend Leon.

"But, Marvin," said Leon, "you're not too old. Plus, you have a lot of experience and common sense."

Marvin knew this was true. He could do the job. He was a hard worker. His employers had all been happy with him. Besides, he did not know the details about training yet. Other people had done it, and so could he.

"Hmmm, maybe I can do it," Marvin thought. "I'll start by talking with my career counselor."

Questions About the Story

1. What are some barriers or problems that Marvin thinks will stop him from becoming a truck driver?

_____

_____

_____

2. What does Marvin have going for him (his strengths)?

_____

_____

_____

3. How can these strengths help Marvin become a truck driver?

_____

_____

_____

4. What does Marvin plan to do first?

_____

Answers

1. he thinks he is too old, that he cannot afford to pay for training, and that he has no time for training   2. he has experience, he has common sense, he is a hard worker, his employers have all been happy with him   3. answers will vary   4. talk with his career counselor

Know Your Barriers and Strengths

In the story about Marvin Washington, you looked at both his barriers and his strengths. Barriers don't have to stop you from doing what you want. They are just problems to be solved.

1. Look at the jobs you listed on each Summary next to the charts (pages 57 and 59). Think about trying to get these jobs. Are there any barriers you might have to overcome?

2. What strengths do you have that will help you overcome these barriers?

A good way to learn more about yourself is to talk with others. Others often see things in you that you may not see yourself.

3. Ask a friend, classmate, or family member to help you list your strengths. What other strengths do you come up with?

4. How can your strengths help you overcome your barriers?

What Have You Learned?

Think about everything you have learned about yourself from the activities in this book. You know more about your own values, skills, and interests. You have found a few jobs that may fit your career path. Do you have a better idea of what you would like your life to be like?

Use the space below to show how you would like your life to be. What things do you want in your life? You can draw, write, or even cut words and pictures out of a magazine and paste them here.

Where to Go from Here

Now you are finished with Book One. You should have a good idea about the kinds of jobs that are right for you. You are the only person who can decide what is right for you. Where do you go from here?

The next steps are in Book Two. You will learn how to choose just the right job and how to get it. In Book Two, you will complete different activities. They will help you make good decisions about your career. They will also help you take action to make those decisions come true.

The Jobs Glossary

The Jobs Glossary is a list of more than 150 jobs. It describes each job. The more you know about a job, the easier it is to decide if it is right for you.

All jobs in this glossary are listed under their job families. The six job families were created by John Holland in the *Self-Directed Search*. The job families are Realistic, Investigative, Artistic, Social, Enterprising, and Conventional.

To use the Jobs Glossary, look for the family of the job you want to know more about. Find the name and picture of the job family. The job titles in each family are listed in alphabetical order.

Jobs listed in the glossary are most likely to be available now and in the future. Most jobs listed are entry level. In many cases, new workers can be trained on the job. However, some jobs require a high school education, GED, or some skills training.

To learn more about these jobs or about others that are not listed, call your state employment office. Your local community college or high school career counseling office can also help you get more information.

There are two sources for the information in the Jobs Glossary: the *Dictionary of Occupational Titles* and the *Occupational Outlook Handbook*. Both of these books can be found in your public library.

Realistic

Animal Caretaker: feed and water animals; walk animals; bathe animals; clean kennels; assist veterinarian; give medicine to sick animals; keep records; answer questions

Appliance Repairer: check for trouble; fix appliances (such as dryer, mixer, toaster); meet people; keep repair records

Auto Body Repairer: fix dents; replace parts; use special tools; use math; follow directions; sand and finish

Auto Mechanic: greet people; find car problems; use hand tools; use special machines; test car parts; oil car parts; fix cars; follow directions; ask questions; answer questions

Bricklayer: build walls or floors; cut brick or stone; read drawings; make work exact; follow directions

Broadcast Technician: install, test, and operate equipment; take and give directions; repair equipment; work under pressure; meet deadlines; know electrical and mechanical systems

Bus Driver: transport people on buses; follow time schedule; drive safely; take fares; answer questions; follow route; keep records; work with all kinds of people

Carpenter: build walls; put in doors; make floors; build steps; use hand tools; use power tools; use math; follow directions

Carpet Installer: use math to measure floors; cut carpet to fit; tack down carpet; use hand tools; use power tools; follow directions; drive truck

Computer Repairer: read directions; put in new machines; put new parts in machines; keep computer working; use hand tools; answer questions; fix computers; keep records

Construction Worker or Laborer: carry tools and materials to carpenters, masons, and other workers; dig trenches; operate machines; clean up job site

Cook: order food; cook food; read and follow directions; clean work area; give directions

Dog Groomer: wash dogs; comb or brush fur; clip fur; cut nails; meet public; follow directions

Electrical Tester or Technician: help make and repair radios, TVs, sonar, computers, and other electrical systems; use test equipment; use special tools; use math to solve problems

Electrician: wire homes and offices; put in boxes; fix breakdowns; use hand tools; use power tools; test lines; follow directions

Electronics Repairer: check electronic equipment; fix electronic equipment; keep log of repairs; read blueprints; follow directions; install equipment

Engine Repairer: find trouble in engine; use special tools to fix engine; test parts; see also Auto Mechanic

Farm Worker: plant crops; harvest crops; run farm machines; tend farm animals

Fish and Wildlife Worker: provide and protect habitat; help people use natural resources without harming them; know and use scientific data and conservation methods for soil, forest, fish, animals, and plant life

Floral Designer: read orders; know about flowers; arrange flowers; use good color sense; start and finish work on your own; talk with customers; work under pressure

Forester Aide: raise tree seedlings; plant seedlings; combat insects; protect trees

Gardener: care for lawns; care for gardens; plant trees and grass; trim hedges; apply weed killer; apply fertilizer; water plants and lawns

Groundskeeper: see Gardener

Heavy Equipment Operator: use big machines to move building materials, earth, or logs; grade out roadways; load earth into trucks

Helper or Laborer: lift and carry goods; clean work area; clean machines; set up machines; do minor repairs; hold tools; take machines apart; wrap packages; do errands; follow directions

Laundry or Dry Cleaning Worker: use washing or dry cleaning machines; mend clothes; take out stains and spots; press clothes; do careful work; work with people; use chemicals; take money and make change

Nursery Worker: plant trees or shrubs; water plants; weed planted areas; trim plants; pot shrubs; feed plants; follow directions; use chemicals

Optician: read and follow instructions; work with people; use math; fit and sell glasses and contact lenses; place orders

Painter: put paint on walls; sand or strip old finish; fill cracks; use hand tools; clean area after work; answer questions; follow directions; use math

Photo Processor: develop film; do careful hand work; use chemicals; use special paper; follow directions

Plastic Machine Operator: tend machines; work with chemicals; load materials into machines; check products for flaws; follow exact directions

Printing Press Operator: run press; do careful work; control inks; check quality of work; clean and oil presses; fix presses; follow exact directions

Security Guard: protect people, buildings, and things; guide traffic; answer questions; follow directions; use special equipment; drive car or van; use two-way radio

Service Station Attendant: pump gas; check engines and tires; clean windows; take money and make change; meet the public

Shoe Repairer: fix shoes; clean shoes; dye shoes; use sewing machine; use hand tools; work with people

Small Engine Repairer: find engine problems; change parts; fix parts; ask questions; read and follow directions; use hand tools; use math

Supply Worker: see Warehouse Worker

Survey Helper: use tools to clear brush; pound stakes; carry equipment; use math; follow directions

Taxi or Limo Driver: drive car or limo; work with people; use radio; read maps; take money and make change; keep fare records; keep car clean and ready

Television Repairer: read work orders; check for trouble; measure voltage; replace broken parts; make service calls; talk with public; keep repair records

Tile Setter: put tiles on walls or floors; use math to measure; cut tiles to fit; clean tiles; use small tools; know about colors

Tire Repairer: change tires; test tires; fix tires; balance wheels; ask questions; follow directions

Truck Driver: load goods; deliver goods; check truck for safety; drive truck; keep delivery records; take money and make change; follow directions; know rules of the road

Upholstery Worker: make new furniture; put new covers on old furniture; put pads on wood frames; use sewing machine; use hand tools; work with people; know about colors; know about fabrics; use math

Warehouse Worker: keep supply records; receive and unpack goods; store and keep track of goods; mark or code goods; take goods to users; follow directions

Water and Waste Water Treatment Operator: run equipment to make water clean; use hand tools; use meters; take and test samples; use computers; deal with leaks and spills; know state and local water rules; use math

Investigative

Chemical Engineer: design equipment; use chemistry and physics to solve problems; help control pollution; develop products that use chemicals

Dental Assistant: help as dentist examines; keep patient's mouth dry and clean; clean tools; take x-rays; keep records; answer questions; follow directions

Dietitian: plan special meals; select foods to meet nutritional needs; teach special diets to patients

Drafter: make technical drawings; use computers; use special tools; use math to make work exact; use technical books

Electrical Tester: check and clean electrical equipment and parts; keep records on equipment; find problems and repair breakdowns; use special tools

Eyeglass Lab Technician: follow doctor's directions; cut and grind glass; put lenses in frames; set dials; run grinder; polish lenses; check work; use small hand tools

Food Tester: check foods to make sure they meet quality standards; use special tools; mark or tag problems

Laboratory Assistant: help doctors, dentists, or other scientists find and identify signs of illness; test for drug levels; measure results of treatments; notice details; keep records and report results

Laboratory Technician: test blood, urine, and body tissues; use microscope and other special tools; use stains and chemicals; do exact work; keep records of results; write reports

Licensed Practical Nurse: care about people; read and follow directions; use math; read dials and meters; write reports and records; feed and bathe sick people

Medical Assistant: greet patients; write patient records; file; answer questions; fill out forms; follow directions exactly; give exact directions

Medical Records Clerk: organize written materials; use computers; use math; learn and use special words; make reports; keep files; type; follow directions

Nursing Aide: care for sick people; make beds; serve food; check vital signs; answer questions; keep records; follow directions exactly

Pharmacy Assistant: mix drugs under direction of pharmacist; follow directions; do exact work; issue medicines; label and store supplies; clean equipment and work area

Physical Therapy Aide: give massages; give heat or sound treatment; help sick or hurt people; give directions; follow doctor's directions; keep records

Physician Assistant: take health histories; give physical exams; give certain medicines; treat minor problems; keep patient records

Radiologic Technician: use x-ray machine to find health problems or treat them; help patients get ready for tests; keep patient records; process x-ray film

Research Assistant: follow directions carefully; use math and theories of science to solve problems; keep records and write reports

Respiratory Therapist: treat and care for people who have trouble breathing; check on machines; measure oxygen level; keep patient records; work under pressure

Scientific Helper: use theories of science to solve problems; use special machines and equipment; use math to measure results; keep records; do exact work

Tax Preparer: use math to figure how much tax is owed; read and keep tax records; meet the public; know tax laws and rules; use calculator

Artistic

Actor/Actress: entertain people by playing a role on the stage or on film; use voice and body motions; memorize parts

Advertising Aide: help sell print or broadcast ads to companies or groups who want the public to buy ideas or things; write ad copy; make drawings or use photos to make products or ideas seem wonderful to the public

Arranger: use harmony to make tunes sound different or better; know and use the special sounds of musical instruments and voices; use music theory

Band Director: know musical instruments; lead musicians during practice and concerts; select musicians; know and interpret pieces of music

Choral Director: lead singers in practice and concerts; know and select music; choose singers

Clown: use special makeup, clothes, props, and body motion to make people laugh; may work with animals; work with other show people; may work with children

Composer: create or write music; know and use harmony and music theory; know about musical instruments

Dancer: express ideas, stories, and sound with body movements; work under pressure; work alone or as a team member; stay in good physical shape

Director: interpret plays or scripts; run rehearsals and auditions; select music and stage sets; use knowledge of voice and acting; work under pressure

Disk Jockey: play records and tapes on radio; make announcements for sponsors; do publicity events; entertain listeners

Drama Teacher: teach acting and stagecraft; coach people who act in order to improve their performance in speaking and motion

Editor: check written or film work of others; decide what to print; supervise writers or reporters; write comments or opinions; work under pressure

Fundraiser: help get money and equipment for social service groups and health programs; write proposals; make contacts with people who have money to donate; research foundations and companies

Graphic Artist: use drawings, pictures, and print to present ideas or products to the public; design ads; use paint, paper, photos, and other media to give information; keep files and records; use math to figure costs

Greeting Card Designer: create new ideas and themes for cards; draw or paint sample cards; work with writers to develop written messages

Instrument Player: play a musical instrument in a band, rock group, jazz combo, or orchestra; read music; use harmony and rhythm

Lobbyist: promote ideas and programs of a special interest group to local, state, or national lawmakers

Makeup Artist: use face paint and makeup to help actor or actress look right for the role being played; work with people; work under pressure; know color and style

Music Teacher: teach people how to read music or play instruments; teach music theory and harmony

Painting Instructor: teach about use of color, paints, canvas, paper, and other media; teach composition and ways of applying paints; work with people

Photographer: use math to figure distance and exposures; use camera and lighting equipment; follow directions; give directions; work under pressure; sell work

Public Relations Worker: help businesses, schools, or other groups present their goods and services to the public; work with TV, radio, newspapers, and magazines to get information to the public; write speeches; make visual presentations

Puppeteer: use puppets, voice, and motions to tell stories

Radio Announcer: introduce recorded music; present news and weather; read ads; operate control board; research and write scripts

Reporter: get information about events and people; organize and give information; write articles or give radio or TV reports; use computers and other special equipment; work under pressure

Sculptor: create images from clay, metal, or stone; sell work; keep records of work and materials

Singer: know and read music; interpret music with voice; practice often

Sketch Artist: use pencil, pen, or charcoal to make drawings of people, places, or objects; use special papers and tools

TV Announcer: write and read news or sports reports; read ads; follow direction; work on community events; meet deadlines; work under pressure

Visual Artist: use art to show ideas, thoughts, and feelings; use paint, pencils, pens, and ink; sell work; draw, paint, sculpt; work under pressure

Writer: use written words to tell about ideas, things, events, and people, either true or made up (nonfiction or fiction); sell work to newspapers or magazines

Social

Activities Leader: plan and lead recreational activities for people; lead fitness programs; plan and lead sightseeing and shopping tours; assure safety; know and use first aid; keep records; write reports

Adult Daycare Aide: help plan and lead activities for older people in a daycare program; serve meals; see that clients take needed medicines; clean work area; help clients with personal care; keep records; write reports

Camp Counselor: lead and teach campers to swim, ride horses, and hike; teach campers how to be safe in the outdoors; give guidance to campers; work with other staff; keep records on campers and activities

Case Aide: give information about services to clients; transport clients; help clients with eligibility rules; give special services to clients; keep records of clients and services

Caseworker: help people cope with problems; work with adults, children, or youths; find and arrange for assistance; keep case records; write reports

Companion: see Private Household Worker

Counselor: help people with personal and career problems; keep records; write reports; refer people to other helpers

Elementary Teacher: teach numbers, music, language, science, and social studies to young children; keep records of children's progress

Employment Interviewer: help employers find the right workers; ask questions; get information from job hunters; match employers' needs with job seekers' skills; keep records on jobs and people

Fitness Club Worker: see Health Spa Attendant

Health Spa Attendant: help customers use the spa; teach exercise, fitness, and bodybuilding; plan personal fitness and exercise programs; keep records

Home Health Aide: give personal care; clean house; wash clothes; cook and serve food; do shopping; give medicine; cheer patient; keep records; make home safe; answer questions; follow directions; report to family; report to doctor

Hospital Orderly: move hospital patients in beds or wheelchairs; care for equipment; help give personal care to patients

Library Assistant: keep books and other library materials in order on library shelves; help people get library cards; check books out to patrons; sort returned books; help patrons with special needs

Lifeguard: supervise swimming pool or beach; watch for and go to help people in trouble in the water; stay cool in emergencies; know and use lifesaving and first aid

Nursery School Attendant: see Preschool Teacher

Nursing Home Aide: care for old people; change bed linens; deliver meals and feed patients; bathe patients

Paralegal: seek facts of a case; write reports; help lawyer in a trial; file papers; review rulings on other cases; keep records; use math; follow directions

Passenger Service Agent or Representative: help people make travel plans; tell people about rates and routes of travel; use math to figure costs; write and sell tickets; keep records

Playground Leader: supervise children; lead games and activities; handle emergencies; keep playground and equipment safe for children

Police Officer: patrol roads and neighborhoods; investigate crimes; catch lawbreakers; direct traffic; give first aid; write reports

Preschool Teacher: greet children; feed children; change diapers; play with children; read stories to children; teach crafts and games; teach music and language; follow directions; help parents; clean play area; keep records

Private Household Worker: plan and cook meals; do laundry; care for children; care for pets; keep house clean; do errands

Probation Officer: work with people in the justice system; counsel and refer clients; check on clients and inmates and help them return to society

Recreation Assistant: teach games to children or adults; teach crafts; teach music; lead exercise classes; give first aid; handle emergencies

Teacher Aide: help students with reading and math; type and file; grade papers; keep student records; order supplies; set up machines such as VCRs and overhead projectors

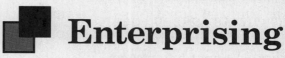

Enterprising

Bank Teller: work with public; cash checks; take deposits and give out withdrawals; count money; sell bonds; sell travelers' checks; keep bank records; give receipts; type data; sort checks and deposit slips; give information about bank services; follow directions

Barber: greet people; cut or trim hair; wash hair; style hair; give permanent waves; color hair; answer questions; keep business records

Cafeteria Worker: greet patrons; take food orders; serve food; tell about special menus; set and clear tables; answer questions

Caretaker: do heavy housework and maintenance; wash windows; wax floors; do light carpentry; paint; mow lawns and do gardening

Cosmetologist: help people look good; wash, cut, or trim hair; style hair; give permanent waves; color hair; give manicures; apply makeup; make appointments; keep records; buy supplies; keep work area clean

Counter Clerk: work with people; take orders; answer questions; take returns; take money; make change; explain terms of sale or rental; write receipts; follow directions

Flight Attendant: get food and supplies ready; greet people; serve food; answer questions; give first aid; help with safety; check tickets; keep records; give directions

Host/Hostess: welcome restaurant guests; be polite; direct guests to coat check; assign tables to guests; escort guests to their seats; give menus; take money and make change

Hotel or Motel Clerk: greet guests; assign rooms; take money; make change; write credit card slips; keep hotel records; answer phone; give information

Insurance Salesperson: tell clients about insurance products; help clients with financial planning; fill out forms; make sales calls; stay in touch with clients

Janitor: clean offices or hotels; fix things; empty trash; use tools; keep supplies; follow directions

Manufacturer's Sales Representative: help sell products to wholesalers and retailers; travel to meet with customers; know about products and prices; help retailers display products; keep records; write reports

Postal Clerk: may meet the public to sell stamps and services; load and sort mail; give information; collect money and make change

Real Estate Agent: help sell or buy homes or other property; know zoning, tax law, and financing; meet the public; use math to figure costs; know the city or town resources; find out about the housing market

Retail Sales Worker: wait on customers; make out sales checks; take money; make change; give receipts; give information about products; stock shelves or racks; mark price tags; take inventory; follow directions

Sales Route Driver: load, sell, and deliver goods to customers; follow a planned route; check stock in stores; arrange shelves or refill vending machines; make small repairs to displays or equipment

Travel Agent: work with public; make hotel and car rental arrangements; plan trips; make travel reservations; give information on travel papers; enter and read computer data; use math; sell services; follow directions

  # Conventional

Baker: mix and bake ingredients for bread and other baked goods; follow written directions exactly; measure ingredients; order supplies; keep work area clean

Bank Teller: work with public; cash checks; take deposits and give out withdrawals; count money; sell bonds; sell travelers' checks; keep bank records; give receipts; type data; sort checks and deposit slips; give information about bank services; follow directions

Billing Clerk: use math to figure costs and fees; read and type data; write bills; keep files; use adding machine; use computer information

Cashier: add bills; take money; make change; fill out credit card forms; give receipts; deal with the public; follow directions

Computer Operator: type in data; follow directions; load disks, tapes, or paper; keep log book; solve error problems; find and correct mistakes

Credit Clerk: check credit history; read loan papers; use math; write letters; talk to employers; keep credit records; follow directions; answer questions

Data Entry Keyer: make neat typed letters, records, or bills; use computer and other office machines; keep track of documents; use good spelling; work with other people

File Clerk: classify, store, update, and find office information; keep track of files loaned; make copies of records; find missing files; use office machines; work with people

Food or Grocery Checker: ring up or scan prices on customer purchases; total the bill, take payment and make change; check I.D.; accept returns and give money or credit for them; wrap or bag groceries; tally cash at end of shift; work under pressure

Inventory Clerk: count products; read codes; mark products; use scanners, readers, or computers; use math and write reports

Mail Carrier: read addresses; sort mail; take mail to houses and offices; pick up mail; pick up money; write notes; answer questions

Mail Clerk: send and sort mail or packages; deliver mail or packages; get mail ready for post office; run machines; read addresses

Messenger: pick up and deliver letters or small packages; drive small truck or ride bike; use two-way radio; follow directions exactly; work in all weather; read maps; keep records

Office Worker: type letters; file; enter data on computer; use copy machine; use other office machines; answer phones; take and deliver messages; follow directions; plan work

Order Taker: receive orders for goods or services; answer questions about goods or services; use math to figure costs; keep records of orders; use telephone; deal with the public

Posting Clerk: keep records of money coming in and money going out; use math to check amounts; make up bank deposits; make or write reports

Quality Control Clerk: check products to see that they meet standards; send items of poor quality back to be made right; keep records; make or write reports

Receptionist: greet callers; direct callers to person who can help them; answer questions; open and sort mail; type and file; answer telephone

Secretary: process and give information to other workers; make appointments; fill out forms; take shorthand; type; file; answer phone calls; keep business records; use office machines

Sewing Machine Operator: sew clothing for children, women, and men on a machine; do one part of garment, or other product, well; add trimmings or buttons; be exact in your work; work under pressure

Small Parts Assembler: put small machine or equipment parts together; notice details and colors; have good eyesight; follow directions exactly

Small Products Assembler: put parts together to meet guidelines; use good judgment; test products; read blueprints; use special tools

Stock Clerk: receive, unpack, store, and keep track of goods; keep records of goods coming in or going out of storeroom; mark codes and prices; bring goods to sales floor

Waiter/Waitress: meet the public; explain menus; take and serve food orders; set up and clear tables; figure bills; make change

Word Processing Operator: type letters; check work for errors; use good spelling; copy handwritten papers; keep file records; file; follow directions

YES	NO	MAYBE
Must have it	Nice to have it	Can get along without it

77

■ PERSONAL VALUES ■	■ PERSONAL VALUES ■	■ PERSONAL VALUES ■
Be free to do what I enjoy	Be happy	Sense of inner peace

■ PERSONAL VALUES ■	■ PERSONAL VALUES ■	■ PERSONAL VALUES ■
Feel good about myself	Have good health	Be liked by others

■ PERSONAL VALUES ■	■ PERSONAL VALUES ■	■ PERSONAL VALUES ■
Have fun in my life	Have no worries about money	Know I did well

■ PERSONAL VALUES ■	■ PERSONAL VALUES ■	■ PERSONAL VALUES ■
Have lots of free time	Be in good shape	Be loving

■ PERSONAL VALUES ■	■ PERSONAL VALUES ■	■ PERSONAL VALUES ■
Be kind to others	**Be in charge of my own life**	**Be honest**
■ PERSONAL VALUES ■	■ PERSONAL VALUES ■	■ PERSONAL VALUES ■
Do what I know I should	**Have others respect me**	**Live in a certain part of the country**
■ PERSONAL VALUES ■	■ PERSONAL VALUES ■	■ PERSONAL VALUES ■
Have an open mind	**Be neat**	**Take risks**
■ PERSONAL VALUES ■	■ PERSONAL VALUES ■	■ PERSONAL VALUES ■
Have time to think	**Be artistic**	

■ WORK VALUES ■	■ WORK VALUES ■	■ WORK VALUES ■
Have steady work	Earn good money	Work indoors

■ WORK VALUES ■	■ WORK VALUES ■	■ WORK VALUES ■
Work outdoors	Travel for my work	Work the same hours every day

■ WORK VALUES ■	■ WORK VALUES ■	■ WORK VALUES ■
Have friends on the job	Have a good boss	Help others

■ WORK VALUES ■	■ WORK VALUES ■	■ WORK VALUES ■
Be part of a team	Learn new things	Know what I am supposed to do

■ WORK VALUES ■	■ WORK VALUES ■	■ WORK VALUES ■
Work flexible hours	Be in charge	Do or make something important
■ WORK VALUES ■	■ WORK VALUES ■	■ WORK VALUES ■
Work with people	Feel good about my work	Work close to home
■ WORK VALUES ■	■ WORK VALUES ■	■ WORK VALUES ■
Do one thing at a time	Work in my own way	Stay busy
■ WORK VALUES ■	■ WORK VALUES ■	■ WORK VALUES ■
Work by myself	Do clean work	Get ahead in my job

■ WORK VALUES ■	■ WORK VALUES ■	■ WORK VALUES ■
Have health insurance	Have vacation and sick days	Do many different things

■ WORK VALUES ■	■ WORK VALUES ■	■ WORK VALUES ■
Use what I already know		

■ WORK VALUES ■	■ WORK VALUES ■	■ WORK VALUES ■

■ WORK VALUES ■	■ WORK VALUES ■	■ WORK VALUES ■

■ PEOPLE VALUES ■	■ PEOPLE VALUES ■	■ PEOPLE VALUES ■
Have lots of friends	**Have close family ties**	**Know lots of people**

■ PEOPLE VALUES ■	■ PEOPLE VALUES ■	■ PEOPLE VALUES ■
Have a good, solid marriage	**Have someone to turn to or talk to**	**Make friends**

■ PEOPLE VALUES ■	■ PEOPLE VALUES ■	■ PEOPLE VALUES ■
Be needed	**Have a few close friends**	**Have family nearby**

■ PEOPLE VALUES ■	■ PEOPLE VALUES ■	■ PEOPLE VALUES ■
Have time to be alone	**Know people I can trust**	**Have a great social life**

■ PEOPLE VALUES ■

■ PEOPLE VALUES ■

Spend money on my friends

Have someone to do things with

Be a good friend

■ PEOPLE VALUES ■

Be a good parent

Be a good son or daughter

Help others

■ PEOPLE VALUES ■

Meet new people

Be independent

■ PEOPLE VALUES ■